"Author David
of his own exp
the rules and cc
us to fix or change the person with same-sex attractions; our place is simply to love them. Just like anyone else, the person with same-sex attractions first needs to hear that his heavenly Father cares for him. Prosen reminds us of the power of affirming love in our own experience. When someone takes the time to just be with us and tells us the truth in a compassionate way, we are more likely to receive it. Each of us, then, as spiritual mothers and fathers, may be a vehicle for Christ's affirming love shining in the loneliness of same-sex attractions."

— **Suzanne Baars, PhD**
Catholic psychotherapist and
founder of the Baars Institute

"David Prosen has written a powerful booklet that I wish every Catholic adult would read. With incredible authenticity and transparency, he takes the reader into the interior reality — so often marked by wounds and pain — of those who experience same-sex attractions. Yet he also points the way to hope and healing in Christ, and the ways the Body of Christ can be a source of healing. This book will change the way you see the world."

— **Dr. John Bergsma, PhD**
Catholic Bible scholar, author, speaker

"With compassion and honesty, David Prosen reveals an empowering vision for sharing the liberating love of Jesus Christ with men and women trapped in the culture's false messaging and still longing for authentic love."

— Lisa Mladinich
Host of Shalom World TV's
WOMAN: Strong Faith, True Beauty

Accompanying Those with Same-Sex Attractions

A Guide for Catholics

David Prosen

Our Sunday Visitor

www.osv.com
Our Sunday Visitor Publishing Division
Our Sunday Visitor, Inc.
Huntington, Indiana 46750

24 23 22 21 20 19 1 2 3 4 5 6 7 8 9

Our Sunday Visitor Publishing Division
Our Sunday Visitor, Inc.
200 Noll Plaza
Huntington, IN 46750
1-800-348-2440

ISBN: 978-1-68192-405-2 (Inventory No. T2298)
eISBN: 978-1-68192-420-5
LCCN: 2018963944

Cover and Interior design: Amanda Falk
Cover art: Shutterstock

PRINTED IN THE UNITED STATES OF AMERICA

DEDICATION

To my mother, who has modeled for me what unconditional love is, and for the many prayers she offered for me daily. Thanks, Mom, for not giving up and losing faith in God and in me as your son. Your faith in the midst of much loss in your life has been a bright beacon of hope to me. I believe your prayers are the reason why I'm still alive, both physically and spiritually. Thank you, Mom. I love you very much.

To my friends Paul, Ron, Ana Lisa, Peggy C., and other loved ones who have touched my heart. We were never meant to live out this journey to Christ alone. It is friends like you who have helped me, inspired me, and believed in me. Your authentic love has been a reflection of Christ's love for me. Thank you.

To my sister, Darlene. I love you so much and miss you daily, even after all these many years. And to all others who have touched my life and are no longer here, especially both my biological father and my stepdad, Joe, who was a good Catholic male role model for me. Eternal rest grant unto them, O Lord, and let perpetual light shine upon them. May the souls of all the faithful departed, through the mercy of God, rest in peace. Amen.

CONTENTS

Foreword

Father John F. Harvey, OSFS, who founded the Courage apostolate in 1980, would often say that "our best ambassadors are our members," men and women who, living with the experience of same-sex attractions, had chosen to pursue the virtues of chastity and friendship according to the mind of the Church. Like Father Harvey, I have a deep respect for these brothers and sisters of ours, who speak very candidly about a profoundly personal experience — often to a skeptical or even hostile world — and testify to the power of God's grace and providence to bring healing, peace, and freedom to their lives.

This kind of testimony is essential in our day, as questions about sexual identity, sexual attraction, and sexual intimacy come up ever more frequently in both secular and Church environments. The design and will of God for sexuality and sexual intimacy, as it is revealed in Sacred Scripture and the teachings of the Catholic Church, is still good news for every human being, even though the call to chastity can seem at first like a sacrifice too daunting to attempt. In a world that so quickly rejects God's plan, however, the Church needs to proclaim it more clearly than ever. Dogmatic formulations, while always true, can sometimes be hard to hear amid the noise of the media and of political discourse. Personal witness captivates the attention of the modern world.

David Prosen is in a unique position to testify to the beauty and goodness of God's will for sexuality and of the Church's call to chastity. As a man who has experienced same-sex attractions for most of his life, he speaks very candidly about his own search for love and acceptance, the compromises he made along the way, and the disappointment he encountered. As a Catholic who has embraced the Church's teachings about chastity, he shares honestly how difficult it once was to hear that teaching, and what a difference it made in his life once he was able to accept it. He is able to lead clergy and others in ministry to a deeper understanding of what Catholics who experience same-sex attractions need and seek from the Church and their spiritual fathers. This book is a special gift to the Church and could not have come at a more important moment.

"The great ideals of the past failed not by being outlived," G. K. Chesterton wrote in *What's Wrong with the World*, "but by not being lived enough. ... The Christian ideal has not been tried and found wanting. It has been found difficult; and left untried." David does not deny that the Christian call to holiness, which includes the call to chastity, can be difficult. But he invites the reader not to stop there — not to reject God's plan, untried, as an impossible ideal. His candid testimony provides important guidance, both for those who experience same-sex attractions and for those who love them, to find a path through the difficulties and arrive at the fulfillment and the joy that God has planned for each of his sons and daughters.

Fr. Philip G. Bochanski
Executive Director
Courage International

Author's Preface

I am a Catholic man who experiences same-sex attractions.

I have found tremendous freedom and peace in embracing the Church's teachings about homosexuality, after many years of fighting the truth. Knowing how much joy life in the truth has brought me, I am troubled when I see shepherds and leaders in the Church promote ideas that contradict Church teaching and condone sin. In an effort to be kind, too many in the Church are embracing cultural thought as fact without proof, presenting the Church's teachings as "mean," and advocating for her to change.

When our shepherds don't speak with clarity, those of us with same-sex attractions who strive to live according to the Church's teachings feel letdown. Thank goodness, these shepherds are the minority. Many others help tremendously, as I have experienced firsthand. They have helped me grow in my relationship with Christ, supported me, encouraged me, and have been Christ to me. These amazing and inspiring shepherds, and others within the Church, provide clarity, truth, hope, and love in a time of chaos, where love is too often equated with simply being "nice."

Those of us who experience same-sex attractions need much more than to be treated nicely. We need to be loved authentically, with truth, and given hope in Christ. I wrote this booklet for priests, bishops, lay leaders, and members of the Church who want an easy-to-reference guide for accompanying and loving their brothers and sisters who bear this particular cross. This booklet is designed to be read easily, and it's packed with concrete ways to help Catholics who experience same-sex attractions, yet seek to embrace the Church's beautiful teachings.

David Prosen
October 2018

I

Are We Asking Ourselves the Wrong Question?

There is much confusion right now in our Church as members attempt to discern ways to love, welcome, and accompany those who experience same-sex attractions. This book is intended to equip bishops, priests, religious, and lay leaders, as well as all members of the Church, with knowledge and concrete strategies for how to respond to and welcome into the Church those who experience same-sex attractions, while authentically loving them as Jesus does.

The *Catechism of the Catholic Church* makes it clear that, regarding those who experience same-sex attractions, "They must be accepted with respect, compassion, and sensitivity" (2358).

How do we respond as a Church to this vital call? Many leaders and members of the Church have loved ones experiencing same-sex attractions and must face this question daily. The struggle to find the balance between loving the person while not condoning unchaste acts is a challenge that some accept. Others disagree with what the Church upholds as truth and want the Church to change her position (as though the Church somehow has the authority to change what is true).

For those in the Church seeking to welcome and minister to those who experience same-sex attractions, many questions arise. Yet I think the questions we tend to ask are missing the point. Maybe the question here isn't the often asked, "How do we welcome and accompany those in the Church who experience same-sex attractions?" Perhaps instead we should ask, "What are the needs of those in the Church who experience same-sex attractions, and how can we meet these needs?"

Needs and Wants

When I think of the word "needs," I think of Jesus' words on the cross: "I thirst." Here is Jesus in his most vulnerable state ever. He has been wrongly accused and sentenced to death, abandoned by his friends, whipped, spat upon, robbed of his clothes, mocked, rejected by most, and left there to hang on a cross in immense pain.

> After this Jesus, knowing that all was now finished, said (to fulfill the Scripture), "I thirst." A bowl full of vinegar stood there; so they put a sponge full of the

> vinegar on hyssop and held it to his mouth. When Jesus had received the vinegar, he said, "It is finished"; and he bowed his head and gave up his spirit. (John 19:28–30)

Many theologians write that when Jesus said "I thirst," he wasn't referring to a physical thirst, but instead to his thirst for our souls. He freely chose the cross because of his thirst for us to be restored to relationship with him. While his physical body certainly thirsted for water, his much deeper thirst was for each one of us. Likewise, he wants us to thirst for him. The psalms are filled with references to the human soul thirsting for God, such as, "O God, you are my God, I seek you, my soul thirsts for you;/ my flesh faints for you,/ as in a dry and weary land where no water is" (Ps 63:1).

The soldiers didn't know that Jesus' thirst was more spiritual than physical, and they gave him vinegar. Now, these soldiers clearly didn't want to meet Jesus' needs, since it's obvious that vinegar isn't going to quench thirst. If the soldiers had done the right thing and given Jesus water, his real need still wouldn't have been met. Why? Because the soldiers assumed his need was something to drink. That's not what Jesus meant, so the soldiers wouldn't have met his true need, even if they had sincerely tried. Similarly, we as Christians might give people what we assume they need, often based on what they tell us they want, when, in fact, it isn't even close to what they need. When we do this, we're more than likely hurting them and not helping them.

There is a huge difference between wants and needs. I want chocolate chip cookie dough ice cream. I need healthy food for my body to live. I want soda pop or sweet tea. I need water for my body to live. If I want to get married to a person of the same gender, ultimately, I might want the Church to change her teaching. Yet, what I really need is to be accepted for who I am as a child of God and authentically loved by others.

Jesus knew what he wanted *and* what he needed, because he was God. The rest of us often don't know what we really need ... we just know what we want. But what we want might not be what is best for us and might even harm us in the long run. We see enticing things in our culture that we want, such as money, fame, power, and even harmful things like drugs or pornography. The more we give in to the desire for these things, the more they distract us from seeking what we really need.

Jesus' words on the cross, "I thirst," provide the key to what each of us really needs. Thirst is a vital need that has to be met, or we will die. When he said "I thirst," he expressed that he thirsts for us like we thirst for water. He longs for us to thirst for him too.

Our culture has a lot of power to influence and shape what we want, and even to convince us that these wants are legitimate needs. But our faith shows us what we truly need: we need a relationship with God and with each other. We cannot survive without God. We need him far more, even, than we need water. This is why Christ compares the spiritual water he gives with the physical water we drink: "Everyone who drinks of this water will thirst again, but whoever drinks of the water that I shall give him will never thirst; the water that I shall give him will become in him a spring of water welling up to eternal life" (Jn 4:13–14).

We also, as members of the Church, need each other. We cannot survive without connections to other people. The Bible is filled with references to how we are to love one another. We need others, and God reveals himself through our interactions with one another.

Starting when I was eighteen years old, I lived as a gay-identified man, and I was rejected by some people in the Church — people I perceived as holy. Some even broke my trust and told others what I had shared in private about my same-sex attractions. I already struggled to realize the authentic love Christ had for me, and these betrayals by my fellow Catholics only made that struggle worse. I *needed* acceptance — to see the love of Christ for me. I *needed* sensitivity and compassion. I *needed* to see the love of Christ in those who professed to be Christians. I needed hope. I needed authentic Catholic/Christian friends who would be there, listen to me, and pray with and for me. Instead, my trust was broken.

Many people in the Church who live with same-sex attractions face these same needs. How can the Church meet these needs? In particular, how can we meet these needs when the people experiencing them are still struggling with *wants* that go against Church teaching?

This is where our commitment to truth becomes absolutely critical. If we discard Church teaching in favor of catering to desires that oppose it, we don't do anyone any favors. On the contrary, we may in fact be causing a great deal of harm. It's important to note that needs are nonnegotiable. This is what distinguishes wants from needs. I can get by if my wants aren't met; in fact, if my wants aren't really good for me, I will be better off without them. But if my needs aren't met, I will not survive.

What Does the Catechism *Say?*

So, to return to our earlier question: What do those who experience same-sex attractions need from the Church?

Actually, the answer is the same for everyone who is struggling to live well on their Christian journey. Whether we experience same-sex or opposite-sex attractions, we all struggle. There are those who are in pain from divorce, or who have had an abortion, or are survivors of a loved one's suicide (and these are just a few examples).

So, what do we need? We need truth. We need authentic love. And we need hope. These three are not wants but needs, all of which must be met in order for our souls to thrive and survive.

The good news is that these three needs are also three beautiful gifts that come from God. In my opinion, these three gifts are intertwined so intricately and wonderfully that each one needs the other to exist. Without truth, we cannot give or receive authentic love, and we have no foundation on which to lay our hope. It might appear to be love because it is nice or the right thing to do, but without truth, there can't be authentic love. Without authentic love, truth is cruel and burdensome, and hope is impossible. Without hope, truth and love lack direction and joy.

So if we want to meet the needs of those in the Church who experience same-sex attractions, we need first and foremost to meet their needs for truth, authentic love, and hope.

Before we begin to explore concrete ways to do this, we need to look at what the *Catechism of the Catholic Church* says on the topic of homosexuality. The sections that discuss homosexuality specifically are paragraphs 2357–2359, quoted in full here:

> Homosexuality refers to relations between men or between women who experience an exclusive or predominant sexual attraction towards persons of the same sex. It has taken a variety of forms through the centuries and in different cultures. Its psychological genesis remains largely unexplained. Basing itself on Sacred Scripture, which presents homosexual acts as acts of grave depravity, tradition has always declared that "homosexual acts are intrinsically disordered." They are contrary to the natural law. They close the sexual act to the gift of life. They do not proceed from a genuine affective and sexual complementarity. Under no circumstances can they be approved.
>
> The number of men and women who have deep-seated homosexual tendencies is not negligible. This inclination, which is objectively disordered, constitutes for most of them a trial. They must be accepted with respect, compassion, and sensitivity. Every sign of unjust discrimination in their regard should be avoided. These persons are called to fulfill God's will in their lives and, if they are Christians, to unite to the sacrifice of the Lord's Cross the difficulties they may encounter from their condition.
>
> Homosexual persons are called to chastity. By the virtues of self-mastery that teach them inner freedom,

> at times by the support of disinterested friendship, by prayer and sacramental grace, they can and should gradually and resolutely approach Christian perfection.

Many believe that the *Catechism* promotes hate, because it refers to homosexual acts as "intrinsically" and "objectively" disordered. Many get very upset about these words. I'll address this in more detail a little later. For now, I want to look at the prevailing wisdom in our culture, which colors the way we perceive the Church's teachings. Our culture accepts and teaches that God created those of us with same-sex attractions this way. So the word "disordered" seems to refer to the full person, not to appetites, attractions, or inclinations. Again, we'll go into more detail later on in this booklet.

If we read the *Catechism* carefully, we do not find hate there. Instead, the whole text urges the faithful to approach the discussion of homosexuality with truth, authentic love, and hope. Here are just a few examples:

> **Truth:** "Its psychological genesis remains largely unexplained."[1]

> **Authentic love:** "They must be accepted with respect, compassion, and sensitivity."[2]

> **Hope:** "They can and should gradually and resolutely approach Christian perfection."[3]

As we begin to explore concrete ways to meet those in the

Church who experience same-sex attractions with truth, authentic love, and hope, it is important to recognize that this is always what the Church urges us to do. Sadly, there are deep divisions not only in the culture, but also within the Church, that make it difficult to proceed. So we will begin by looking at the problem in our Church and the root of our division, so that we can seek truth together.

II

The Root of the Church's Divide

For years we've been bombarded with messages in our culture from activists and those who identify as LGBT. These messages have caused much confusion. Sadly, this confusion has seeped into our Church. I've seen well-intentioned priests with a strong desire to welcome those who identify as LGBT abandon the Church's teachings on chastity — teachings that apply to all Christians. These shepherds believe that loving and welcoming people with same-sex attractions in the Church means brushing aside or even outright ignoring her teachings.

Yet a growing number of Catholics who experience and/or struggle with same-sex attractions don't identify as LGBT. We're not the loud voices heard in the media today. Instead, we're usually the quiet whispers heard in the confessional, those who come to our local parish seeking spiritual direction, advice, or support. We are striving to follow the Church's teachings on sexuality and to pursue wholeness through holiness by growing in virtue. There is joy in this and, ultimately, we're talking about growing closer to the Creator of the universe, our heavenly Father.

Sadly, many of us in the Church who experience same-sex attractions feel isolated and alone. As we live — or attempt to live — a chaste life, we find ourselves ridiculed for doing so. Yes, many do not speak about their struggle for fear of being condemned. Yet, there are also a number of those who don't speak about their struggle for fear that they will be told they are wrong to live a chaste life. It can be very discouraging and scandalous to be told by a priest or lay leader that the Church is wrong on the topic and may soon change her position. Sound extreme? This has happened, and some have left the Church as a result.

Our culture loudly proclaims that the truths upheld by the Church about human sexuality (and homosexuality) are harmful. We're told Church teaching causes emotional pain and contributes to suicide. Sadly, there are some who have felt suicide was their only option and have acted on this, after feeling rejected by family or society. But such rejection of a person with same-sex attractions is not what the Church teaches. That is a tragic misrepresentation of the Church's position. In fact, my own experience and that of many others show that depression, despair, and suicidal thoughts are actually the result of living the LGBT life, not the fruit of trying to live by the Church's teachings.

In my own experience, I was miserable living the LGBT culture as a gay-identified young man. I sought out someone to love, and it was difficult to find. In the first year or two, I found myself sleeping with almost a hundred men — and I wasn't even trying to be promiscuous at this point. I felt lonely and desperately went to bars several times a week hoping to find "Mr. Right." What I found was heartbreak, relationships that didn't last, and even violence. I was traumatically raped in one of my very first relationships at age eighteen.

Although I did not attempt suicide, I often thought about not wanting to live. I was filled with overwhelming loneliness and intense shame. I self-medicated with alcohol and drugs. Later, I used promiscuous sex not only to numb the pain but also in hopes of being held and feeling cared about. This only worsened the shame. When I was twenty-four, my younger sister died unexpectedly just after turning twenty-one. I remember thinking it should have been me, since I was the one passively killing himself by driving while intoxicated and having promiscuous "unprotected sex" in the middle of the AIDS crisis.

Sadly, those promoting the LGBT agenda refuse to believe that many of us were miserable, even suicidal, while pursuing an active LGBT life. That simply doesn't fit the narrative. Instead, we're told that we aren't being true to ourselves and that it's impossible and harmful to live a chaste life as the Church teaches. These messages are troubling when they come from our culture; when they come from people within the Church, they can be devastating.

A Question of Identity

What is at the heart of this confusion, even inside the Church? It is the insidious lie that equates *attractions* with *identity*. This slickly packaged falsehood has been promulgated so adeptly and gained such tremendous traction that few stop to question it or seek research either to back it up or refute it. The falsehood is this: those who experience same-sex attractions, or those who identify as LGBT, are created that way.

You've probably heard that before, haven't you? In fact, you've probably heard it a lot. You probably even know some people who have been attracted to members of the same sex for as long as they can remember. I experienced this as well, and believing I was born that way was easy to accept. In fact, it exonerated me. God made me that way, so how could it be wrong?

As a Church, we need to navigate this area carefully as we attempt to help.

The Church faces deep internal tension in her attempts to welcome those who experience same-sex attractions and accompany them on their Christian journey. On one end of the spectrum are those who discard or ignore Church teaching in their attempts to show compassion. On the other end are those who are only focused on condemning homosexual acts, without compassion for those experiencing such desires.

As Christians, we are called to love all people, and that includes those who experience same-sex attractions. This doesn't mean we should condone behaviors that are contrary to Church teaching. To do so ultimately risks the loss of souls. Being politically correct is the nice thing to do, of course, but simply being nice is not an act of authentic love. Instead, being nice can be a way to avoid making others angry. If our actions are based on avoidance or fear, then likely they're coming more out of self-protection than authentic love. As a Church we need to act out of love, not fear, and focus on what's best for each precious human person.

Many Catholics and Christians refer to homosexuality as "same-sex attractions." There's a reason for this. Words such as gay, lesbian, and even homosexual are labels, which insinuate that this is an identity. Yet the experience of same-sex attractions is not an identity. Ultimately, treating same-sex attractions as a person's identity causes much harm to many in our culture and in our Church.

In an article I wrote, "I am not Gay, I am David," I speak of the question that's often at the center of debate on this topic: "Did people specifically choose these particular attractions, or did God make them this way?"[4] The problem is that these are two separate questions and shouldn't be treated as an either-or requiring us to pick one or the other. Instead we need to consider both questions separately.

First, do people who experience same-sex attractions specifically choose these particular attractions? Most people do not choose which sex they will be attracted to. So the answer to this question of choice is almost always a resounding "no."

Now we look at the second question: Did God make them this way? When considered as an either-or dichotomy, the answer to this question must be "yes." But the truth is that the answers to both questions can be "no." The fact that most people don't choose the attractions they experience is not proof that God made them this way.

NBC News[5] and others have written articles based on LiveScience's work[6] documenting that homosexuality is natural in the animal world. Many argue that this suggests homosexuality is a natural phenomenon, which means same-sex unions for human beings should not be looked down on or forbidden. I would counter this argument with another "natural" example: female black widow[7] spiders and female praying mantises[8] are both known for killing their sexual partner after mating. It's natural for these two species and might be biological. Since it happens elsewhere in nature, does this mean it would be okay for human beings to kill sexual partners after having sexual relations? Of course not. We need to consider our actions on a whole different level, as human beings have been created with two gifts animals do not have: reason and free will.

There is no scientific proof about whether people are born this way or not. In fact, the American Psychological Association website states:

> There is no consensus among scientists about the exact reasons that an individual develops a heterosexual, bisexual, gay, or lesbian orientation. Although much research has examined the possible genetic, hormonal, developmental, social, and cultural influences on sexual orientation, no findings emerged that permit scientists to conclude that sexual orientation is determined by any particular factor or factors.[9]

Fr. James Martin's recent book, *Building a Bridge*, has stirred up controversy within the Church on this very topic. During an interview about his book, he was asked what he would say to one who is LGBT and struggling. He replied: "God made you this way. You are wonderfully made, just like Psalm 139 says. You were knit together in your mother's womb this way. ... This is part of your identity."[10]

It is troubling to see such a statement from a Catholic priest, because there is no proof that this is true. Yet many in our culture and in our Church have not only accepted this as a truth but preach it as well. "Andrew" from Courage International uses a comical analogy to explain how identities based on attractions don't fully explain who we are:

> Imagine you are holding a hamburger in your hands and it started talking to you. You might be a bit surprised, but just pretend that you would listen to what he had to say. Now imagine it telling you who "he" is... and he says "I'm ketchup" or "I'm pickle" or "I'm beef patty" or "I'm gluten" or "I'm calories" and so forth. How would you respond to these statements by the talking hamburger? (Aside from saying Oh my gosh! A talking hamburger!) The point for us to consider is that even though all of those facets of the hamburger are true, none of them are able to reflect the *fullness* of who that hamburger really is.[11]

In other words, our identity isn't wrapped up in the attractions/inclinations we experience or in our particular sexual/romantic appetites. There's so much more to who we really are, and this is true of all of us, whether we are attracted to people of the same sex or the opposite sex. Our identity is in Christ. We are men and women created in the image and likeness of God. That is our only true and authentic identity.

III
The Gift of Truth

Truth has become a relative term in our culture today. My truth is my truth. Your truth is your truth. There is no objective truth. So, when it comes to topics such as homosexuality, there can be much confusion, and we are seeing this in our churches.

The good news is that truth is not relative. There is objective truth. Our Church's teachings are based on this objective truth. It's not politically correct, and we might not even like it, but it is still objective truth. We cannot change it to be the way we want it to be. Pilate asked, "What is truth?" when Truth himself was standing right in front of him. We can be confused and blinded to Truth just as Pilate was if we aren't looking at the reality of Truth: it's not merely an abstract idea; it is a person, Jesus Christ.

Since the topic of homosexuality causes intense emotions, many ask, "How do we know these teachings are true?" It is helpful to briefly review how we as Catholics discover the truth. This is one of the beautiful aspects of our Catholic faith. The *Catechism of the Catholic Church* states:

> It is clear, therefore, that in the supremely wise arrangement of God, sacred Tradition, Sacred Scripture, and the Magisterium of the Church are so connected and associated that one of them cannot stand without the others. Working together, each in its own way under the action of the one Holy Spirit, they all contribute effectively to the salvation of souls.[12]

If I were to give ten people the same Bible verse to read, it's very possible that they would have ten different interpretations, especially if it's a long verse. The Church helps us ensure that objective truth does not get chiseled down into a half-truth. Tradition, Scripture, and the Magisterium are intertwined through the Holy Spirit. This is why we can count on the teachings of the Church to be true and not biased by anyone's individual interpretations or experiences.

Disordered?

As I mentioned earlier, many think the Church hates homosexuals because it describes homosexual tendencies as being "intrinsically" and "objectively" disordered. This is partly because the word "disorder" in the secular sciences usually refers to a psychological or emotional problem. But what does the Church mean by this term as it is used in the *Catechism*?[13] To answer this, I want to look at the 2006 US Conference of Catholic Bishops' document "Ministry to Persons with a Homosexual Inclination: Guidelines for Pastoral Care." While I encourage you to read this insightful document in its entirety, there are three excerpts in particular that beautifully explain what "disordered" means:

> 1) The homosexual inclination is objectively disordered, i.e., it is an inclination that predisposes one toward what is truly not good for the human person. Of course, heterosexual persons not uncommonly have disordered inclinations as well. It is not enough for a sexual inclination to be heterosexual for it to be properly ordered. For example, any tendency toward sexual pleasure that is not subordinated to the greater goods of love and marriage is disordered, in that it inclines a person towards a use of sexuality that does not accord with the divine plan for creation.[14]
> 2) It is crucially important to understand that saying a person has a particular inclination that is disordered is not to say that the person as a whole is disordered. Nor does it mean that one has been rejected by God or the Church.[15]
> 3) Nevertheless, while the particular inclination to homosexual acts is disordered, the person retains his or her intrinsic human dignity and value.[16]

It is important to note that the terms "order" and "disorder" refer strictly to what God has authored into creation. It doesn't have to do with what feels natural, what comes easily, or what is observable in behavior. Nor does it refer to a person's identity. If we forget that, then, of course, "disordered" sounds hurtful!

As Catholics, it is important that we fully understand the Church's teachings so we can remove confusion and bring clarity. The light of truth can clear our blindness, but it will take patience on our part. Many have intense emotions such as anger about the term "disorder" being used in the *Catechism*. If you're seeking to minister to those who experience same-sex attractions, it is important for you to understand that this anger isn't an attack on you. It isn't necessarily an attack on the Church, either. It is more than likely a defensive reaction, because these individuals believe that they are being attacked by the Church. So it's up to us to help them see the truth: the Church loves them authentically and wants what is best for them, in keeping with the way God made them.

Anger and Truth

Many people didn't like Jesus because he spoke truth. And since he asks us to pick up our crosses and follow him, it stands to reason that we also will not be liked by many as we speak truth.

The first time I heard that masturbation was a grave sin, I was very angry and didn't believe the person who told me. At that point in my life, I had finally accepted that the act of homosexuality was a sin. However, I believed masturbation was okay and even necessary to help keep me from sexually acting out. I even practiced masturbation without fantasy and thought I wasn't lusting, since I focused only on the pleasure of the act.

But I couldn't help but wonder: what if that guy was right,

and masturbation was a grave sin? I asked God to show me the truth. And in his time, he did. I eventually read in the *Catechism* that masturbation is considered a grave sin.[17] I was still angry and still struggled to accept this. I thought the Church was wrong. I wrestled with this and wrestled with God. It didn't seem fair. I felt sorry for myself and thought: "It's hard enough to accept that I can't be in a relationship, and now you're telling me not to masturbate? Not even occasionally, to relieve pressure so I can stay celibate?"

The wrestling match continued, as I fought against the truth in the *Catechism* and, ultimately, God. But it was this wrestling match that helped me come to the truth. I learned that masturbation is still an act of lust, whether I fantasized or not. The *Catechism* clearly defines lust, and it is not just about fantasies or the desire for sex: "Lust is disordered desire for or inordinate enjoyment of sexual pleasure. Sexual pleasure is morally disordered when sought for itself, isolated from its procreative and unitive purposes."[18]

I couldn't argue with this. Masturbation was wrong. Finally, totally exhausted, I conceded the match. Even though it didn't make sense to me and seemed unfair, I admitted that I was wrong and God was right. I repented and asked for forgiveness. It was at this point, and only at this point, that I could finally ask God, sincerely, for help to stop. And that is what he was waiting for from me. He needed me to ask.

And then my eyes were opened. Masturbation, lust, and sexual acting out were all keeping me from growing closer to my God. When we sin, no matter the sin, we are turning our back to God. Once I let go of this sin, I began to desire to be closer to God, to turn toward him and grow in holiness, self-control, chastity, and true authentic charity. This is what truly fills our hearts with joy: pursuing and striving to grow in virtue and holiness. Why? Because this is what we were created for.

God doesn't force himself upon us. He has given us free will. He wants to shower his graces upon us; but until we are open to receive them, these graces won't penetrate our hearts. When I sincerely repented and asked for the graces I needed to live chastity fully, my heart was finally ready to receive those graces.

For those in the Church seeking to minister to people with same-sex attractions, know that they need to hear the truth. They might not like it, they might not agree with it, and they might even experience unpleasant emotions. But they need to hear it, and the Church has a real duty to proclaim the truth.

Sadly, we don't hear much about the truth of chastity — for those who experience same-sex or opposite-sex attractions — taught in our churches. It is critical that leaders and members of the Church understand this beautiful call to chastity, a call we all share. How can we convey this truth to Catholics who experience same-sex attractions if we don't fully believe it or appreciate it ourselves? The virtue of chastity is often misunderstood and overlooked; yet, it's needed now more than ever during this confusing time in our culture.

The truth is that God calls each of us to chastity. It doesn't matter if we experience same-sex attractions, opposite-sex attractions, whether we are married, single, religious, or in a relationship. All of us are called to chastity. Chastity is an important part of our identity in Christ. Chris Stefanick, in the film *The Third Way*, says this about chastity: "It's not about saying no to pleasure or no to herpes and no to hell. … It's about saying yes to one important thing … yes to authentic love."[19]

It's an amazing feeling when we give a gift to someone we love and the recipient is deeply moved or happy as a result. This is what happens when we give God the gift of ourselves. We are made in his image and likeness. God could have made us robots who do his bidding, but he gave us free will. He wants us to choose him out of love. This includes giving him everything about us, such as our desires, sexual appetites, emotions, successes, and failures. He appreciates all the gifts we give him, including our sexual desires. These desires were given to us for a reason, and he longs for us to unite these desires to his will, by using them as a gift of self in a marriage between one man and one woman. It gives God joy when we choose to give our whole selves to him, and this can be a cause of profound joy for us as well — even more incredible than when we give a meaningful gift to a friend or family member. I know for myself that now that I have given my whole self to God, I experience an inner peace that I never knew when actively living out the LGBT life.

Our God is a God of hope, love, and truth. The Church he instituted exists to mediate every grace we need to live a Christian life of virtue and to overcome our sinful inclinations and struggles. It's her very purpose. With the help of these graces, living a chaste life is not only possible, but also empowering. For many Catholics who experience same-sex attractions, we find our lives to be filled with joy when we strive to live chaste lives. Living in truth sets us free to be fully who God created us to be, rather than accepting a false identity based on our desires and inclinations.

So how do we as Catholics uphold the truth while loving and welcoming those struggling to live it? The answer is to speak the truth in love, just as Christ did. In John 4, we read that Jesus met a Samaritan woman at the well and had a beautiful conversation with her about the living water he gives. This conversation is important not only because of what Jesus said, but also because of the cultural tensions that existed between Jews and Samaritans at the time. The Jewish people viewed the Samaritans as a lesser race, and they wanted nothing to do with them. Yet Jesus, a Jew, cared about the Samaritan woman, talked to her, and connected with her in authentic love — even when he had to tell her some hard truths about herself. At one point he told her to get her husband. She told him she didn't have one. Jesus told her, "You are right in saying, 'I have no husband'; for you have had five husbands, and he whom you now have is not your husband; this you said truly" (Jn 4:17-18). He didn't try to cover an uncomfortable situation with "niceness," telling her that it was okay for her to have had so many husbands and to be living with a man she was not married to. He spoke truth to her. Yet because he spoke the truth in love, she could hear it and receive it.

This is the key. When we seek to welcome and accompany those who experience same-sex attractions in the Church, we're really seeking to help them grow in their relationship with Christ. Rules don't change people — they are meant to guide us. Only authentic love changes people; without love, the rules, no matter how rooted they are in truth, become chains.

For the Samaritan woman, the truth set her free. She ran back into her village and told everyone she met about Jesus. It was his compassion and love that strengthened her, enabling her to embark on a life of grace in union with him. One might wonder whether she slipped into sin again at some point. Old habits do tend to die hard. Yet, Jesus is patient. At the same time, he is always clear: sin no more. He spoke truth to her, and his compassion emboldened her to share the Good News. Now she knew she could return to the fountain of mercy, to receive the grace needed to avoid this sin in the future. This is true for all of us. The more we are able to return to Christ and ask for mercy, the stronger we grow in holiness and virtue. This speaks volumes about the Church's mission today.

Truth Saves Souls

When I was about twenty-one years old and actively living as a gay-identified man, I went to a priest for help. He told me that I could be in a relationship with a man and have sex if I loved the man. I asked him about the Scriptures that condemned acts of homosexuality. He told me that many laws in Leviticus are no longer applicable. They were instituted to protect us in biblical times, but we don't need them now. He gave the example of not eating pork, which back then was dangerous to eat but is safe today because we know how to cook it. He told me that homosexuality had once been forbidden because we needed to procreate, but today it's not as important, since there are parts of our world that are overpopulated.

Years later, I learned that the restrictions and laws not applicable to us today are those that aren't moral laws. Those that deal with morality can never be changed. It would be similar to saying the Ten Commandments are no longer applicable to us, when in fact they're just as relevant today as they were when the

Lord instituted them through Moses.

Dr. Jean C. Lloyd addresses pastors in a beautiful article that also pertains to any of us who minister to others in our Church. I think her words can also pertain to family members or parents of those who experience same-sex attractions. She writes: "Continue to love me, but remember that you cannot be more merciful than God. It isn't mercy to affirm same-sex acts as good. Practice compassion according to the root meaning of 'compassion': Suffer with me. Don't compromise truth; help me to live in harmony with it."[20]

When the priest told me that I could have sex with a man whom I loved, I experienced a gnawing feeling in my heart that it was wrong. I ignored this feeling and continued doing what I was doing, and I was miserable. I guess this is why it is important for us to make sure we don't confuse "the Church" with "the people of the Church." What the Church teaches cannot err, but individuals within the Church can be very confused and misleading.

Years later, when I learned the truth and how to live in harmony with it, I was no longer miserable. In fact, I remember after I stopped living an active gay life, a liberal friend of mine said to me: "David, I can't believe how much better you are. I think there is nothing wrong with being gay. I would never tell this to anyone else, but this is working for you. You are so peaceful now." What did she see? She saw the Holy Spirit at work and the true peace that comes when we pursue a life of chastity.

God has made us in his image and likeness. To live according to that image and likeness includes chastity. He longs for us to live chaste, pure lives; to imitate him; and to grow in him. For those of you reading this who are priests and deacons, I encourage you to speak on this in homilies. All of us need to hear that chastity is something *all* of us are called to, and it *is* possible for all of us.

IV
The Gift of Authentic Love

How do we show authentic love and not condone sin? Some of the following is taken from a free e-book titled *Mom, Dad I'm Gay. How Should a Catholic Parent Respond?*, which I co-authored with Allison Ricciardi.[21] Although it's addressed to parents of children who experience same-sex attractions, much of the information can be applied to anyone, and that includes both leaders in the Church and individual members.

If someone discloses to you that he or she experiences same-sex attractions, be fully present and listen. That is one way to show your love. Try to understand where the person is coming from. What has this been like? How long has this person felt this? What is his or her understanding of it? Don't try to speak, just listen. This is not the time to preach. There will be time later to plant seeds.

Next, affirm the individual's courage and express how much you appreciate him or her sharing this difficult revelation with you.

Now that you've listened and sought to understand where the individual is coming from, take it to prayer as soon as possible. It is important to pray and not react. Instead of reacting, take a step back and ask God for the wisdom to know what seed (or two) to plant. In some situations, you might discern that you need to say something over the next few days. In other cases, you may need more time to discern, especially if emotions are intense. In that situation, it's okay to say: "You have known about this and have been dealing with this for a long time. This revelation is new to me, and I need a little time to process this and pray about it." Depending on your relationship with the person, you might need a few weeks. Each person is different. There is no cookie-cutter approach to this, because we're all individuals with different experiences. Ask God how he wants you to handle this.

Planting Seeds

In my own experience, I can say that I am grateful for the many seeds planted by my mom and loved ones. At one point while I was living the gay life, a friend of mine who was a deacon invited me to come back to the Catholic Church. I told him I couldn't because I was gay. He suggested I go anyway, but also pray and sincerely ask God to show me his truth. My friend was right. If we ask God to show us the truth, and we're sincere in wanting that truth, then I believe God will show it to us ... but in his time.

In my case, the journey took a long time, and I certainly didn't make it all at once. I eventually stopped having promiscuous sex and decided that I would raise my standards for a committed relationship. That didn't work either and ended badly, since he didn't share my faith. As a result, I raised the bar again, this time promising myself I would only date a Christian gay-identified man to whom I was attracted, who shared similar values and beliefs. I never found him.

As this happened, I began to yearn more for God and his truth. One day, I felt him say to my heart, "Yes, David, you never chose this attraction, but you can choose whether you act on this or not."

My deacon friend had planted a seed of love and truth. That seed and others planted by my mom and other friends slowly took root. It took a while for these to grow, but they did.

As you plant seeds, make sure your words and suggestions are not coming from your emotions. Instead, they should come from the Holy Spirit. To be clear, emotions can help us if we use our reason and think it through before choosing an action. But in this case, let your action be prayer. Pray and ask God what to say. Tell him you're unsure, because you don't want the walls to go up. He knows what that person needs to hear and the precise moment when it is needed. When it's time, you will feel nudged to say something.

Another important thing: don't bombard a person with books and films or lectures. That would be like opening a case of seed packets and dumping them all in one place. Planting a seed is small. It might be three words or a sentence or two. The longer you speak, the more you risk being perceived as lecturing, and walls might go up. Then, nothing will be heard.

It's very possible that the person might get angry after you plant a seed. Emotions are normal. While I am grateful now for the seeds planted in my life, sometimes I was angry or frustrated when certain things were said to me. I was furious when I was told that masturbation was a grave sin. I needed to be. That anger helped me look for and wrestle with the truth, until finally the seed began to sprout and grow and flourish into a beautiful plant.

Whether you are a priest, lay leader, church member, or family member, it's not your job to change or fix others. Your job is to love them. It's God's job to do the rest. Remember, as Jean Lloyd writes, compassion means to "suffer with" someone.[22] This is a part of authentic love. Jesus did this for us — he models what it means to love by carrying his cross for us.

Walking in someone's pain and avoiding the temptation to take their pain away is very difficult. Yet all of us humans need our crosses. If we let him, God can use those crosses in amazing ways for our healing and salvation. We can't fix or change anyone except ourselves, but we can stand by others in their suffering and suffer with them.

1. Authentic Love and Gender Wounds

Emotional wounds can be very deep and very painful. These wounds leave scars that affect how we view ourselves. Some can impact us at the most intimate level, affecting our femininity or masculinity, and these wounds happen to many (if not all) individuals, regardless of which sex a person is attracted to.

I am a counselor, and I remember working with a new client who was the stereotypical "macho man." He was the sort of person who might appear frightening even when he wasn't angry because of his mannerisms, vocal tone, and facial expressions. He came to see me because he struggled with sexual addiction and an unquenchable urge to sexually objectify women. To be clear, this man didn't experience same-sex attractions at all. It was extremely difficult for him to come in to counseling, let alone to disclose the problem he struggled with — yet he did. When I affirmed his tremendous courage, determination, and strength in coming in for help and taking the risk to share this with me, he began to weep. He explained that he viewed himself as weak and not masculine at all. His vision of his masculinity had been deeply distorted by past wounds.

I share this so that you can see the profound effects of wounds to one's gender, regardless of sexual attraction. These wounds can cause us to believe lies about ourselves. As a result, many of us face negative consequences and adopt unhealthy coping skills to numb our pain. Even more devastating, these wounds can prevent us from seeing our true identity.

As mentioned earlier, our identity is not the attractions or inclinations we experience. Nor is our identity what we do for a living or hobby. Our identity is in Christ. Our identity is being a man or woman created in God's image and likeness. This is important: a man or a woman. When we begin to chip away at sexual differences, we are attacking a key part of who we are in Christ. Men need to be affirmed in their masculinity, and women in their femininity. This isn't a want; it is a need.

Yet our culture does not affirm masculinity or femininity. In fact, there is a growing movement to remove masculinity or femininity from any discussion of identity. Some are even trying to change our language, replacing the pronouns "he," "she," "him," or "her" with "they." Even more extreme, there is a movement to incorporate a whole slew of new pronouns[23] into our dictionary and, ultimately, our conversations, operating on the principle that gender is a choice we make.

Affirmation of one's masculinity or femininity has become unacceptable in public schools, Scouts, and other children's activities and educational environments. In addition, kids and adults are bombarded with false messages about sexuality in the media, from TV and movies, to news outlets, magazines, and books. As a Church, it is important that we affirm people in their true sexuality (as designed by God), beyond gender stereotypes.

I also want to say a word about transgenderism. It is crucial to affirm a person's sense of masculinity or femininity before that person accepts a false identity of transgender. Once an individual has embraced a transgender concept as his or her identity, it can be very difficult to affirm true sexuality. When a person has embraced a transgender identity, we can and should still show that person love by praying, planting seeds, listening, loving, and accepting that person as a child of God. Here it is also helpful to remember that we can't change anyone. Only God can. Our job is to make sure that whatever we say or do reflects love in truth, and we must pray in hope for healing and conversion. (This is largely outside the scope of this book, but is still an important discussion. For more see the suggested resources in the Appendix.)

Wounds from Childhood

Many boys and girls feel rejected by their same-sex peers and think that they are different and don't belong. Often, those who experience same-sex attractions may have likes and dislikes that are more common to the opposite sex. For example, girls might not be interested in playing with dolls and would rather play with cars, while boys reach for dolls or want to play "house." Same-sex peers sometimes pick up on these differences and tease, which can cause growing shame.

For those who work with children and teens — whether as teachers, coaches, mentors, volunteers, or in any other capacity — pay attention to teasing. If you see little ones or teens (male or female) being teased, called names, and isolated as a result, take some time to talk to them. Ask them whether they are okay and let them know what you saw. Affirm them by letting them know that it wasn't right and that the name(s) they were called aren't true. Normalize their likes and dislikes and help them see that liking or disliking activities doesn't define who they are.

Many (though not all) adult men who experience same-sex attractions say that they were teased as children. Many of them were the kids who were always picked last for sports teams. For many boys, this can lead to a strong drive to "prove" people wrong. For others, it leads to more shame. Instead of thinking, "I can do this and will prove them wrong," they might believe they are too different and can never learn. There were many times I sat by myself watching and not participating as a young boy. An intense shame kept me from taking the risks and learning the skills needed for sports. I believed I was different and not good enough, and many of my peers reinforced this belief for me daily. Years later, after therapy, I looked back and realized that I was a masculine boy who loved roller coasters, climbing trees, adventures, pirates, monsters, and more. It's just that no one ever affirmed me in these preferences.

For those of you who are coaches or volunteers working with boys' sports programs in schools, camps, or churches, you are in a unique position. If you see a boy sitting by himself, connect with him and ask him why he is sitting alone. He might tell you that he hates that particular sport. Ask him what it is that he hates about it. He will probably tell you that he can't play very well. At this point, ask whether he would like you to show him some tips and teach him some of the skills. Another possibility is to assign students who are skilled in sports to mentor others who lack skills or confidence. Offering encouragement may mean everything to a boy. Help him see that not playing sports well doesn't mean he is different. Help him find something that he does enjoy that will affirm his masculine identity, such as climbing trees, adventures, etc. Calling out these traits can help him see the truth that he does belong to the male world. That sense of belonging is extremely important.

It is very common for little girls to be interested in activities that are associated with masculinity, such as getting dirty, climbing trees, or playing sports. Many girls also prefer boyish clothes, such as jeans and sweatshirts, over dresses and other clothing typically associated with femininity. These girls have been referred to as "tomboys." That name can be hurtful to some girls and cause shame. Others don't take it personally and eventually develop feminine-associated interests and clothing preferences. There is nothing wrong with a girl liking sports or preferring jeans to dresses. There can be something wrong if a little girl experiences shame and thinks something is wrong with her because she's interested in these things.

When it comes to affirming young people in their masculinity or femininity, it is important for boys to have male mentors and girls to have female mentors. Boys need to be welcomed into the world of men and shown how they fit there. Girls need to know that they belong to the feminine world, and to have their feminine traits affirmed and appreciated.

These discussions are very important, and making time to have them is an act of love. Reaching out and normalizing young people's experiences or affirming them in their masculinity or femininity can have a tremendous impact.

Biological Reactions Are Not Sins

As a coach, volunteer, or even as a priest, you might hear individuals say that they think they are gay or lesbian. It is important to help them see that these labels are an incomplete picture, as attractions aren't related to one's identity. There is also another important component to this that you should communicate: sexual attraction, whether it is to the opposite sex or the same sex, has a biological component to it. Often, if I had to talk to a guy whom I perceived as good-looking, I felt things like butterflies in my stomach, sweaty palms, an increased heart rate, and tingles. Sometimes I even stuttered. These are bodily sensations, normal biological reactions — not sins. But to one who experiences shame, these sensations can feel like sin. It's critical for us in the Church to help people understand where their moral responsibility lies. It's the acting out of masturbation, sexual fantasizing, pornography, or sex outside of marriage between one man and one woman that is a sin. This is especially important for young people going through puberty, as they're already confused by the changes happening in their bodies and emotions.

Wounds in Adulthood

While many wounds to masculinity or femininity occur in childhood, these wounds can also occur in adulthood. As members of or leaders in the Church, it's important that we be aware of our speech. Are we destroying someone's spirit by making fun of him or her for being different? Attacks to a person's sense of masculinity or femininity can be quite harmful, especially if a person already suffers from wounds in this area.

I remember that while I was attending college in my forties, a female friend made fun of me for putting moisturizing lotion on my dry skin. She mockingly said that men don't do that. (I guess she thought that I should be in pain from chapped, dry skin resulting from severely cold weather and allergies.) It reminded me of the teasing and comments that I received from others while growing up, reinforcing my belief that I wasn't like other males. Thankfully, as an adult I had the logic and confidence not to take her comments too seriously, at least in the long run. At the same time, her comments did hurt at first. We need to be careful in our speech, not just with children but with adults as well. We don't know all that someone may have experienced, their inner wounds, or their perceptions of themselves. It is never good to poke fun at another person's sense of masculinity or femininity, as we simply have no way of knowing what core wounds we're probing, often with innocent intentions.

2. Authentic Love and the Father Wound

Before diving into this and the following section, I want to address those of you who are parents. There is no perfect parent. We are all human, and each of us makes mistakes. There is no perfect child, either. I am sure that your child has made decisions you disagree with. Perhaps your child has said hurtful things to you. It is important to remember that wounds occur when one **perceives** *that one is being hurt, even if there was no malicious intent on the part of the person who gave the wound. For example, I might be thinking about a situation at work and have a frustrated or worried look on my face. A friend who notices this might assume I am looking at him or her with disapproval. Without even realizing it, I may have caused a wound.*

Moreover, there is no consensus on the causes of homosexuality. Many believe it is a mix of nature (predisposition) and nurture. It's important to note that when I discuss father and mother wounds, I am discussing perceptions. Please don't beat yourself up and blame yourself if your child experiences same-sex attractions. You don't know the whole story. Only God does. If you did commit a sin and haven't asked for forgiveness, then I encourage you to do so, both from your child and in the beautiful Sacrament of Reconciliation. If you have already taken this to God and your child, then it's important to forgive yourself and let go. Don't blame yourself for something that may have very little to do with you.

Parts of this section are specifically addressed to priests and seminarians who are discerning the priesthood. This chapter is also important for fathers and those in mentor roles, including catechists, youth ministers, spiritual directors, ministry leaders, and friends or family members.

In the movie *Courageous*, one man asks his buddies, "When did you first think of yourself as a man?" Most of his friends don't know for sure, but one man does. He says, "When my father told me I was."[24] This man found out from his father that he belonged to the masculine world and that he had what it takes.

Many people suffer from father wounds. The sources of these wounds aren't limited to fathers; they may include mentors, teachers, pastors, authority figures, or any men who in some way played a father role. These wounds occur in men and women, regardless of whether they're attracted to members of the same sex or the opposite sex. But many who experience same-sex attractions also suffer deeply from father wounds.

It is difficult to understand the unconditional love of the heavenly Father when one has wounds from earthly fathers or father figures. This can be a barrier to our relationship with God, since it's hard for us to trust in something we have never experienced before. Fathers and father figures have an awesome opportunity to show people what the heavenly Father's love for us is like. Sadly, many people today have seen few examples of this.

My father was an alcoholic who physically and emotionally abused me while I was growing up. He had a lot of unresolved anger, and as he went about his work at home, he would slam things and swear. He was talented in landscaping, woodworking, and fixing up old cars, and as I grew older, he tried to pass on this knowledge to me. But every time he ended up losing his patience, screaming curse words, and calling me names.

As I later learned, he didn't know how to express his love for me, because he wasn't shown how by his father. How can one give something he doesn't possess?

Years later, as I grew closer in my relationship with Christ, I still struggled to see God as my heavenly Father who loves me unconditionally. Thankfully, with perseverance in prayer, frequent reception of the sacraments, therapy, developing healthy coping skills, and finding good priests and support, I began to receive this gift of love from the heavenly Father. The chain has been broken. I am now able to pass on the love that wasn't given to me by my earthly dad, because I have received it from my heavenly Father.

It is critical for those of us in the Church to meet people with same-sex attractions with the love of the heavenly Father. How do we do this?

Priests

First, I want to address priests for just a moment. Your vocation automatically puts you in the role of father. Many of you have already reflected the heavenly Father's love and may not have realized this. We often touch people's hearts without realizing the true impact of what the Holy Spirit has done through us. I think this is especially true of priests. What are some conscious ways you can strive to reflect the authentic love of the heavenly Father? One important way is in the confessional. In that sacrament, you're standing in the place of our heavenly Father. Through the Holy Spirit, you have the unique opportunity to show us his authentic love.

Other important places to demonstrate the Father's love are in spiritual direction, in your homilies, when you give us the Holy Eucharist, when you speak to us privately, when you offer encouragement or correction, and even when you read the Gospel during Mass. You have many opportunities to reflect the heavenly Father's love for us. I have experienced this many times from different priests who have affirmed me as a child of God and as a man. When this happens, it's as if God is hugging me, saying, "David, you are mine, and I love you so much." Don't underestimate the power of God and the healing that he can provide to others through you as a Catholic priest.

Showing the Love of the Father

And it's not just priests who can reflect the Father's love. Each of us as lay leaders and members of the Church can and should reflect that love as well. The challenge is to find ways to show love and acceptance without condoning sinful behaviors.

Men and women who experience same-sex attractions need to be shown the love of the Father. How can you show them this love? I suggest looking first to the Bible. There are many Scripture verses that speak about the love of the heavenly Father. If you have any favorites, share those. Which verses speak God's love to your heart? My all-time favorite is Isaiah 43:4: "Because you are precious in my eyes and honored, and I love you." I first encountered this verse several years ago while reading Fr. Larry Richards' *Be a Man,* and it went right to my heart. Isaiah 43:4 is now the anchor of truth that I hang on to when chaos is around me, or when I experience doubt that the Creator of the universe loves me.

What else can you do to show the love of the heavenly Father? Think of examples you have seen of loving earthly fathers. Personally, I've seen inspiring and emotionally moving examples of earthly fathers in public places such as in church. I have seen them show acceptance and be fully present and attentive to their children. I believe these examples are just a small taste of what the heavenly Father's love for us is like.

Even though many people have wounds from their biological fathers, no one is ever too old to have a father figure in his life. Especially if you work in a pastoral role in your parish or in other mentorship capacities, you have the wonderful opportunity to reflect the heavenly Father's love to the people you serve. Nothing is impossible for God, and he can do amazing things with your efforts and make them his own. Ask yourself: How can you provide acceptance to those to whom you minister as valuable human beings and children of God?

When you speak with people with same-sex attractions, recognize that they often struggle with shame, and shame can be a big barrier. It may take much effort on your part in being real with them to break through the shame, but keep trying. If you persevere, they may eventually be able to receive your acceptance. Don't give up on them. Strive to be fully present and attentive. The message a person gets when another human being actually listens and makes eye contact is, "I matter to this person."

When ministering to people who experience same-sex attractions, the most important thing is to let them know that God the Father loves them. He loves them more than they could possibly understand. I speak from personal experience when I say that men and women who experience same-sex attractions need to hear this. Often, we are caught up in our pain, thinking our struggle is a punishment or that we aren't doing something right. We need help to see the truth that God does love us, that he's not punishing us, and that the attractions we experience are not, in and of themselves, sin. Most importantly, God has not abandoned us, and he never will.

3. Authentic Love and Mother Wounds

The following is intended specifically for mothers, religious sisters, and other female leaders and role models, such as teachers, catechists, youth ministers, mentors, friends, and family members. As with father wounds, there are many ways in which mother wounds occur. Again, these perceived wounds do not necessarily come from our biological mothers. They may also come from other family members, teachers, religious, or any woman who has played a formative role in our lives. Again, bear in mind that wounds occur when someone **perceives** *that he or she has been hurt, even if there was no malicious intent on the part of the person who gave the wound. As I stated in the previous chapter, it is important that you do not blame yourself if your child experiences same-sex attractions. You don't know the whole story. Only God does. If you did commit a sin and haven't asked for forgiveness, then I encourage you to do so, both from your child and in the beautiful Sacrament of Reconciliation. If you have already asked for forgiveness from God and your child, then it's important to forgive yourself and let go. Don't blame yourself for something that may have very little to do with you.*

Dr. Timothy Lock, in an article he wrote for the Love in Truth conference held in Rome, Italy, in 2015, noted that conflicts and absence of one's mother are common experiences for many men and women who experience same-sex attractions.[25] It is important to note that acknowledging these wounds isn't to say they are the cause of anyone's same-sex attractions. As mentioned previously, the APA states that there is no consensus on causes. Still, it is important to recognize and acknowledge wounds that can affect all of us, no matter which sex we are attracted to.

Some men speak of perceiving their mothers as overprotective or domineering. As a result, to take just one example, some weren't encouraged to take risks in sports or other activities. I know some men and women whose mothers were not available due to addiction. Others were emotionally or physically abused by their mothers. Still other men and women were abused by their fathers or others, and are angry with their mothers for not protecting them, as was the case for me.

It took many years for me to recognize that I was angry with my mom. When I was very young, I perceived that she abandoned me in a moment of great terror, and that left a deep wound, though I later learned that she never intended to abandon me. Even when I did finally admit it, I minimized it. I knew I was angry with her, but I pushed it deep down inside, because I also knew that I loved her very much. I felt as though my anger was wrong, a betrayal of someone I loved. Over time, my anger became an obstacle to my relationship with her. The anger in and of itself wasn't bad (emotions are morally neutral), but I perceived it to be and didn't deal with it. This choice allowed the anger to hurt not just me, but my relationship with my mom and with other women.

As members of the Church, we have a particular obligation to help people deal with their mother wounds because the Church is our Mother. Women play a very special role in this healing. How can you help those who are hurting, especially those experiencing same-sex attractions, deal with mother wounds?

Healthy Nurturing

First, offer nurturing love in a healthy way. Women have a natural tendency to nurture, and this is a good and beautiful thing. As women in the Church, whether religious sisters, leaders, mentors, or family members, you can show your love by being fully present and listening, by being nurturing, and by showing empathy and compassion. Mother wounds often cause people to feel that they were never loved, so your presence and sensitivity help prove their value. By providing a compassionate, nurturing presence, you can help a person see what a healthy mother is, reflecting the true compassion that our Church offers at the same time.

I know that this idea of a woman being more fully nurturing than a man is not politically correct. This is not to say that men can't be nurturing, since some can be very nurturing. But most men aren't hard-wired to nurture in the same way as women. Glenn T. Stanton, writer and director of Family Formation Studies at Focus on the Family, discusses the research that proves this, citing numerous studies that discuss differences in the way men and women are hard-wired.[26] One of the most compelling sources he discusses is a book by Simon Baron-Cohen, called *The Essential Difference*.[27] While the book looks at differences between the sexes in light of autism, the author, a professor of developmental psychopathology at the University of Cambridge, begins his book: "The female brain is predominantly hard-wired for empathy. The male brain is predominantly hardwired for understanding and building systems."

It is generally difficult for a woman to see someone else in pain, especially if she has a relationship with that person. (This can be difficult for men, too, but because men and women are wired differently, this impacts women in a profound way.) It's important to understand, however, that nurturing doesn't always mean taking away someone's pain. It does mean being willing to accompany and suffer with another person with true compassion.

Mary, our heavenly mother, is a wonderful example of this. Mary knew that her beloved son would suffer. Yet, she didn't try to rescue him or protect him. She loved him enough to let him make his decision to sacrifice himself. She didn't throw herself on the mercy of Pilate or try to stop this injustice. She knew who Jesus was, and she knew that he was choosing to do the will of the Father. So she stood by his side and suffered with him to the end. I can only imagine the suffering Mary experienced as she watched her son, disfigured by blood and open wounds, carry the cross, and then watched soldiers hammer spikes into his hands and feet.

It takes incredible strength to nurture and empathize while not letting it take you down. We can use Mary as a tremendous model for how to do this. She didn't despair, although she was in immense pain. She grieved, she hurt, and she prayed. She never gave up on God, knowing that he was ultimately in control. That is strength. And you can model that to us.

V

Ways to Show Authentic Love

Many of us in the Church who experience same-sex attractions suffer from deep wounds as a result of sexual acting out. This is especially true for those of us who were promiscuous. I certainly experienced this. In my quest for a man who would love me for me, I found myself doing things I never thought I would do. Memories of things that I did and things that were done to me haunted me, even after I committed to living a chaste life. I would surrender the memories to God, but the shame and self-loathing continued to grow and became an obstacle to my receiving Christ's love for me. I knew God had forgiven me, but there were moments of trauma that needed healing before I could finally let go and forgive myself.

Scatter Shame

When ministering to those who experience same-sex attractions, listen for shame. As it is often said, guilt is an emotion stemming from the belief that "I *did* something wrong," whereas shame is a deep painful feeling coming from the belief that "I *am* something wrong."

Yet the Church teaches that our actions and our sins do not define who we are. Our heavenly Father did not make us to live in shame. He made us out of his love, to live in his love. Jesus Christ has washed us in his blood, and we are made clean. When we sin, we have the Sacrament of Reconciliation to restore us to a right relationship with our heavenly Father. But many of us still hold on to the past and feel shame. Some have also experienced trauma, such as rape, and blame themselves when they weren't responsible. Listen for the shame and, if you hear it, shine the light of truth on it. Shame grows in the darkness like fungus. It cannot withstand the light of Christ.

"I Thirst"

On the cross, Jesus said, "I thirst." He thirsts for each one of us, right now. Reminding people who experience same-sex attractions of this reality can be a profound way to help them see God's deep love for them. One resource I highly recommend sharing is a meditation by the Missionaries of Charity Fathers, entitled "I Thirst for You."[28]

This meditation is powerful, emotionally moving, and it just might melt the hardest of hearts and remove some of the barriers preventing them from seeing how much God does love them. No matter what the immediate results are (or aren't), this can be an amazing seed to plant.

Genuine Affirmation

In his book *Born Only Once,* Catholic psychiatrist Conrad Baars speaks about the importance of affirmation.[29] Genuine affirmation, according to Baars, isn't a list of positive statements we tell ourselves or others (such as, "I'm good and loved," or "You're a good person"). Instead, affirmation is a state of being. Ideally, all children need to experience affirmation from their parents. Affirmation is when parents allow themselves to be fully emotionally moved by the goodness of their child and to communicate it back in such a way that the child knows it's true. This is communicated in many ways, including facial expressions, caring eye contact, acceptance, vocal tone, and other acts that demonstrate unconditional love.

Sadly, as Baars points out, many adults were unaffirmed by their parents. The result is often stunted emotional growth. The unaffirmed adult still needs to be affirmed, and this is where our role as Catholics — especially those who serve in ministry — is so important. When it comes to ministry to those with same-sex attractions, remember that father and mother wounds are often present, which indicates that the person you are ministering to may have been unaffirmed as a child. Genuine affirmation can help bring about healing to these individuals. We can provide affirmation to those we meet by being fully present to them and communicating that they are loved unconditionally as a brother or sister in Christ. Many people expect guidelines on how to do this, but it is more about being than doing. To learn more about genuine affirmation, please check out the book *Born Only Once.*

VI
The Gift of Hope

Many of us in the Church who experience same-sex attractions, who are either living chastely or attempting to do so, are told by our culture that we are harming ourselves. We do not receive encouragement from our culture and, unfortunately, many of us aren't receiving it in our churches either. It is difficult to have hope that living the Church's teaching is not just possible but even good and healing if we don't hear it.

What do I mean by hope? The *Catechism of the Catholic Church* states, "Hope is the theological virtue by which we desire the kingdom of heaven and eternal life as our happiness, placing our trust in Christ's promises and relying not on our own strength, but on the help of the grace of the Holy Spirit."[30] When I speak of the gift of hope here, though, I am not referring to the theological virtue, although it is related to it. What

I mean by "hope" is a sense of knowing or trusting that what one longs for can happen. It's light in the darkness by which we can see. It's the possibility of achievement, or of growth, or of obtaining what one needs. Hope makes the impossible possible, which is why it is related to the theological virtue. When we give encouragement to our brothers and sisters, we are giving them the gift of hope. We are believing in them because of the faith we have in God. When we have faith in them, this might pierce their hearts, leading to confidence in God and in themselves if they rely on him.

Those of us who experience same-sex attractions and want to live as Jesus teaches need to hear that chastity is possible and good. We need hope that this is possible and that the Church isn't asking us to do something unreasonable or unachievable. We need to be told that we *can* do this and that it doesn't mean living a life of desperate loneliness and isolation. We need people in the Church to share this message with us, to combat the despair and discouragement the culture throws at us. We need encouragement from leaders and members of the Church that living as Christ asks won't lead to misery, but will make us truly happy. And we need to be reminded that our hope lies in Christ. A huge part of this is allowing us to see the hope that you have in Christ and the hope that you have in us as we surrender to him.

One of the most powerful vehicles of hope and encouragement I have found in the Church is Courage International.[32] No matter what our cross is, the Christian life can be hard sometimes. It's even harder when we think we have to do it all alone. Courage International, which is for men and women who experience same-sex attractions and strive to follow the Church's teachings, provides community and support so we don't have to do it alone. Courage International is grounded in the hope that living according to the Church's teachings is not only possible, but also deeply fulfilling and meaningful. Words cannot express how empowering it is to know that I am not alone in this journey and that I have brothers and sisters who truly understand, support, and pray for me. This organization has given me the gift of hope, and I strongly recommend it.

If there is no chapter of Courage in your area, and if you are a priest or know a priest who might be willing to start a chapter, contact the Courage office. They will help you get one started. If it looks like having a chapter in your diocese isn't a possibility, there are other options for individuals seeking the support that Courage offers, such as conference meetings through Facebook or connecting via the email list.

I also recommend EnCourage, the sister organization of Courage, which is for family members and loved ones of those who experience same-sex attractions. In addition, Courage International has created a website specifically for bishops, priests, deacons, lay leaders, health care workers, and lay people called Truth and Love,[33] which is filled with wonderful information to help you in your ministry.

Hope and Healing

For a long time, I begged God many times a day to cure my same-sex attractions, yet the attractions persisted. A friend of mine suggested that maybe God wasn't curing me because there was nothing wrong with being gay. It took a long time, but when I finally came back to God and accepted the Church's teachings,

I felt a peace in knowing that this was a cross. I stopped asking for a cure and instead sought God more deeply, asking him for strength to live chastely and to know him more personally.

It turns out God didn't want to "cure" me — he wanted to heal me. One of my first experiences of healing happened when I attended a retreat through the University of Steubenville. Two men gave the men at the retreat a talk on what it means to be Catholic men of God. They spoke in deep, loud voices and related everything in football terms. By the end of the talk, I was furious. As I prayed about my reaction, I realized that I had never let go of my anger toward the male peers who taunted me while growing up. I was projecting my anger onto these speakers. In fact, I'd projected that anger onto many other men throughout my life. I forgave my childhood peers, knowing that forgiveness is a process and not something that happens immediately.

A short time later, at Mass, I asked God what he wanted me to do about the two men who spoke at the retreat. I opened my eyes and looked to my left, and there, kneeling next to me, was one of the two guys. Very funny, God. But then the words "sign of peace" came to my mind. I realized at that moment that this was a truly beautiful gift from God. That sign of peace wasn't just a symbol to my neighbor; it was real reconciliation.

The healings didn't stop there. I developed some good male Catholic friendships and mustered the courage to ask two of them who loved baseball to teach me how to throw, catch, and hit. Slowly, I began to get better and gain some confidence. I surprised myself by agreeing to play every Sunday in an informal coed softball game with the graduate and nontraditional students. It was challenging, and I had to fight my memories, but by doing so I began to develop more confidence and additional healing from my past.

The healings have continued over the years. One of my favorites came about after working with a life coach about ten years ago. I joined a gym and was still terrified of the locker room. The old emotions and thoughts from high school came back to haunt me. To be clear, I never thought I was a woman, but as a young man I also never felt like I was a man. I used to view myself as a subspecies. My life coach asked me to participate in the locker room, to shower and to change and notice where I fit as a man in this environment for men.

I felt a sense of panic when I first walked in. I imagined someone would scream at me to leave, to say I didn't belong. This wasn't logical, of course, but the panic was real. I was shocked that it didn't happen. Instead, several men spoke to me. This was life changing for me. At this point I realized that I do, in fact, belong to the world of men. Praise God! This was huge for me. I began to learn that I had always possessed good masculine traits.

My healing journey continues. I just finished seeing a Christian therapist who was helping me to gain healing over shame and to embrace the truth about who I really am as a child of God. To be clear, this isn't "reparative" therapy. It is Christian counseling, and much healing has occurred with this therapist.

Am I cured? No. In fact, I don't like that word. I still experience same-sex attractions, but I have received a number of healings that continue to bring peace to my heart. In the past, if someone asked who I was, I would have said I was a gay man. Today, I know that's not my identity. There is so much more to who I am. Who am I? I am David, a Catholic man of God.

The Healing Journey

It is important to remember that all healing comes from God, but very often he chooses to heal us through the natural means at our disposal. This includes therapy. When helping people in the Church who experience same-sex attractions, you can encourage them to seek out counseling. I'm not talking about therapy to change one's sexual orientation. I am talking about therapy to help bring about God's healings from wounds in our life that block us from fully living out his will. There is so much hope when we're able to let go of the past and look with joy to the future. Chastity-focused counseling approaches, as well as working on wounds from the past, can bring much peace.

Please be aware that secular therapists will encourage those who experience same-sex attractions to accept this as an identity. I strongly recommend that you point people to Catholic or Christian counselors, even if the goal of therapy has nothing to do with same-sex attractions. I remember going for grief counseling after the death of my father, and I accidentally mentioned that I had same-sex attractions and was living chastely. He told me, "You can be in a gay relationship and be Catholic." When I disagreed, he stated, "I'm Catholic. I know this is true."

As you seek to minister to those in the Church who experience same-sex attractions, keep in mind that change is a continuum. Some people who experience same-sex attractions have no decrease in the attractions, but they continue to live a chaste life. This can be considered healing, especially for those who were addicted to porn, masturbation, sex, or relationships. Others find same-sex attractions decrease a little bit as they strive to live the Church's teachings, while for others the attractions decrease dramatically. I even know people who are now married with fulfilling lives after living as an identified LGBT individual in the past.

Some argue that same-sex attractions never go away completely. Actually, I believe the reality goes deeper. After all, we all experience attractions to people of the same sex, just not sexual ones. All of us are attracted to other people. Even when seeking friends, we tend to gravitate toward those we are attracted to, not just physically, but on a personal level. Maybe I like that my friend possesses a strong virtue of courage. Or maybe I am attracted to a person's sense of humor, their compassion, their smile, their talents, their intelligence, or just how I see Jesus in that person's eyes. It is completely natural to be attracted to people, and this includes people of the same sex. We are naturally attracted to the good.

I believe this is one explanation as to why same-sex attractions don't completely dissipate. A person who doesn't experience same-sex attractions might notice that a person of the same sex has a nice smile and not think twice about it. But for the person who experiences same-sex attractions, such an observation can lead to feelings of shame, which might even trigger eroticized attractions. This is especially true for those who have acted on same-sex attractions in the past. Yet attractions in themselves, whether to persons of the same sex or the opposite sex, are normal and good, as we are all attracted to the good. If, as a leader or a member of the Church, you speak to someone who shares experiences like this with you, normalize them. Speak of how there is beauty in everything that God has created — and it is good and normal to be attracted to what is good. If need be, refer the individual to a good Catholic or Christian therapist to seek any healing that may be needed. (See Appendix for a resource that might be helpful in locating Catholic therapists who support the Church's teachings.)

Conclusion

It takes much courage for people to seek help regarding same-sex attractions, whether for themselves or loved ones. Many of us have been hurt by turning to those who don't embrace all the Church's teachings and encourage us not to do so. Others have felt attacked and condemned by people in the Church who simply pass judgment on us because of our attractions. As a Church, we need to ensure that anyone who comes to us for help in this matter will encounter truth, authentic love, and hope. To provide this, we need first of all to pray that God will show us the ways we can provide these gifts to meet the true needs of those in our parishes and communities who experience same-sex attractions. If we are open, God will guide us — after all, he loves his children more than we could ever imagine, and he wants to help us give them what they truly need. Our job isn't to fix anyone, nor is it our duty to condemn. Instead, we need to meet people where they are, sow the seeds, and trust that God in his mercy will bring about healing if we let him.

Appendix
Further Reading

Help and Accompaniment

Courage International, https://couragerc.org/

Encourage, https://couragerc.org/for-families/

Truth & Love, https://truthandlove.com/

Jason Evert, The Chastity Project, https://chastity.com/

For Catholic therapists near you that support Church teaching, visit www.catholictherapists.com

The Kings Men offer an experiential healing weekend for men (not specific to same-sex attractions but for men regardless of the struggle). For more information, visit www.intothewildweekend.com

Born Only Once: The Miracle of Affirmation, by Conrad W. Baars, MD, edited by Suzanne Baars (2016)

The Courage to be Chaste, by Fr. Benedict Groeschel, CFR

Made for Love: Same-Sex Attraction and the Catholic Church, by Fr. Michael Schmitz

Living the Truth in Love: Pastoral Approaches to SSA, edited by Janet E. Smith and Fr. Paul Check

Documentaries on Same-Sex Attractions and the Catholic Faith

Desire of the Everlasting Hills, directed by Erik Van Noorden, www.everlastinghills.org

Invited to Courageous Love: The Catholic Church and Homosexuality, produced by Courage International, www.couragerc.net

The Third Way: Homosexuality and the Catholic Church, directed by John-Andrew O'Rourke, http://www.blackstonefilms.co/

The Church's Teachings on Transgenderism

Ryan T. Anderson, "When Harry Became Sally," Love and Fidelity Network, December 21, 2017 (video of lecture)

Jason Evert, *The Chastity Project* videos, available at YouTube.com

Robert A. J. Gagnon, "How should Christians Respond to the Transgender Phenomenon?" *First Things,* (October 16, 2015)

An interview with Walt Heyer, "Speaking Out About the Transgender 'Delusion,'" *National Catholic Register,* May 6, 2015 (written by Brian Fraga). Walt Heyer lived eight years as a woman following "gender reassignment" surgery before undergoing therapy, turning to Christ, and returning to living as a man. His website, SexChangeRegret.com, is designed to support people who regret changing genders.

Prayers and Inspiration

Courage International, "Prayers and Spirituality," available at https://couragerc.org/resources

Missionaries of Charity Fathers, "I Thirst for You"

Notes

1. *Catechism of the Catholic Church, Second Edition.* (United States Catholic Conference of Bishops), 2357.

2. CCC, 2358.

3. CCC, 2359.

4. David Prosen, "I Am not Gay, I Am David," *Lay Witness Magazine*, January/February 2011, 26. https://www.lifesitenews.com/opinion/i-am-not-gay-i-am-david.

5. Sara Goudarzi, "Gay Animals Out of the Closet?" NBC News, November 16, 2006, http://www.nbcnews.com/id/15750604/ns/technology_and_science-science/t/gay-animals-out-closet/#.W8f-hLmhKgdX.

6. LiveScience Staff, "Gay Animals: Alternate Lifestyles in the Wild," *LiveScience*, September 20, 2011, https://www.livescience.com/16138-gay-animals-bonobos-dolphins.html.

7. Ed Yong, "How Male Widow Spiders Avoid Being Cannibalized During Sex," *National Geographic*, September 20, 2016, https://news.nationalgeographic.com/2016/09/animals-spiders-black-widows-cannibals/?user.testname=none.

8. Carl Zimmer, "This Can't Be Love," *The New York Times*, September 5, 2006, https://www.nytimes.com/2006/09/05/science/05cann.html.

9. "Sexual Orientation and Homosexuality: Introduction (What causes a person to have a particular sexual orientation?)," American Psychological Association, accessed December 17, 2018, http://www.

apa.org/topics/lgbt/orientation.aspx.

10. Joseph Sciambra, "Father James Martin: LGBT Catholics have been treated like dirt. We can do better. Jesuitical Podcast," filmed June 16, 2017, https://www.youtube.com/watch?v=PZ44d-kEAXkE.

11. "Andrew" from Courage International, https://couragerc.org/resource/open-hearts/

12. CCC, 95.

13. CCC, 2358.

14. "Ministry to Persons with a Homosexual Inclination: Guidelines for Pastoral Care," United States Conference of Catholic Bishops, November 14, 2006, http://www.usccb.org/about/doctrine/publications/homosexual-inclination-guidelines-pastoral-care.cfm.

15. Ibid.

16. Ibid.

17. CCC, 2352.

18. CCC, 2351.

19. John-Andrew O'Rourke, dir., "The Third Way: Homosexuality and the Catholic Church," Blackstone Films, 2014.

20. Jean C. Lloyd, "Seven Things I Wish My Pastor Knew About My Homosexuality," *Public Discourse: The Witherspoon Institute*, December 10, 2014, http://www.thepublicdiscourse.com/2014/12/14149/.

21. Alison Ricciardi and David Prosen, *Mom … Dad I'm Gay: How Should a Catholic Parent Respond?* (Huntington, NY: The Raphael Remedy, 2013), https://theraphaelremedy.com/mom-dad-i-m-gay/.

22. Lloyd, "Seven Things."

23. "Gender Pronouns," Lesbian, Gay, Bisexual, Transgender Resource Center, University of Wisconsin Milwaukee, accessed October 19, 2018, https://uwm.edu/lgbtrc/support/gender-pronouns/.

24. Alex Kendrick, dir., *Courageous* (Culver City, California: TriStar Pictures, Sherwood Pictures in association with Provident Films and Affirm Films, 2011), DVD.

25. Timothy G. Lock, Ph.D., "How to Increase Respect, Compassion, and Sensitivity for Individuals with Same-Sex Attraction: Understanding the Latest Research from the Psychological Sciences." Speech at Living the Truth in Love: An International Conference and Resource Event to Address Pastoral Approaches toward Men and Women with Homosexual Tendencies, October 2, 2015, https://rcdop.org.uk/documents/2018/3/Rome%20Conference%20Program_8.5x11_pp1-52_low%20res-1.pdf, pp. 37–41.

26. Glenn T. Stanton, "The Science Says the Google Guy Was Right about Sex Differences," *The Federalist*, August 11, 2017, http://thefederalist.com/2017/08/11/science-says-google-guy-right-sex-differences/.

27. Simon Baron-Cohen, *The Essential Difference: Male and Female Brains and the Truth about Autism* (New York: Basic Books, 2003), 1.

28. "I Thirst for You," Missionaries of Charity Fathers, accessed December 17, 2018, http://www.mcfathers.org/i-thirst-for-you.html

29. Conrad W. Baars, M.D., *Born Only Once: The Miracle of Affirmation* (Chicago: Franciscan Herald Press, 1975), 31.

30. CCC, 1817

Acknowledgments

First, I want to thank my heavenly Father for loving me, blessing me, and calling me to be one of his voices of hope. Thank you, Father, for your healing and for never giving up on me, especially during the times when I had given up on myself.

Second, thank you to my friends John Laney, Melissa Girard, Allison Ricciardi, Mary W., Hudson Byblow, and Ann Schneible of Courage International, who all helped by taking the time to read and offer suggestions and feedback.

Third, thank you to Fr. Philip Bochanski, for both reading my booklet and writing the beautiful Foreword despite your busy schedule. I am very appreciative and touched that you made this a priority. Also, thank you Father, for being a true shepherd to those of us in Courage International. Thank you for your courage in being a voice for us and speaking the truth in love with much clarity.

Fourth, thank you so much Dr. Suzanne Barrs, Dr. John Bergsma, and Lisa Mladinich for your support, taking the time to read this booklet, to reflect on it, and for your very kind words and endorsements.

Fifth, I want to thank the many priests who have shown me truth in love. Thanks for showing me that, as God says in Is 43:4, "You are precious in my eyes, and honored, and I love you." Thank you for being fathers to me and reflecting the heavenly Father's love. You did this in confession, in personal talks, encouraging me homilies, and more. Thank you for your "yes" to God.

Sixth, thank you to Mary Beth Baker and all of the staff of Our Sunday Visitor for believing in the importance of this message and helping me make this booklet a reality.

About the Author

David Prosen holds an MA in counseling from Franciscan University of Steubenville. David was the leader of the Steubenville chapter of Courage from 2004 to 2011. He is an author and a speaker who gives numerous presentations across the country on same-sex attractions from a Catholic perspective. David has given his testimony at the "Living the Truth in Love" conference and in the documentary *The Third Way: Homosexuality and the Catholic Church* by Blackstone Films. David is a lover of roller coasters, enjoys performing in theatre, and deeply loves his Roman Catholic Faith. He has a devotion to Our Lady of Guadalupe, which ultimately led him to where he is today in sharing the truth, authentic love, and hope we find in Christ.